I CAN'T LIVE UP TO YOU

Marcellus J. Vinson

MILTON & HUGO L.L.C.
4407 Park Ave., Suite 5
Union City, NJ 07087, USA

Website: *www. miltonandhugo.com*
Hotline: *1- 888-778-0033*
Email: *info@miltonandhugo.com*

Ordering Information:
Quantity sales. Special discounts are granted to corporations, associations, and other organizations. For more information on these discounts, please reach out to the publisher using the contact information provided above.

Library of Congress Control Number: 2025916139
ISBN-13:   979-8-89285-599-0   [Paperback Edition]
                   979-8-89285-635-5   [Hardback Edition]
                   979-8-89285-597-6   [Digital Edition]

Rev. date: 08/15/2025

Contents

Freshman Year: Insecure

Mother's Dream

My mother wants best for her kid
As any mother should
And I love her for it
But I'm not ready for high school
When I'm not ready to be anything

I didn't realize I was growing up
Till I realized I was growing
That one day I'll living on my own
Left out in the world to find my home
I'm not ready for high school

So you gave me an objective
Become a RN but don't think about it
Worry about what's in your way
At the end of the day you're born for success
But I feel like high school is where I'll fail
I'm not ready

In movies it's painted out as a place that nitpicks your
insecurities
I've got too many to pick on
I was never accepted to be myself
How will I be accepted here?
How am I expected to make it past 4 years
In a school that'll break me down into
Less than atom

I'm afraid
Of confronting new faces
I'd rather be stuck with the ones who forced me to
mask mine
I'd rather stay where I hurt
Than be somewhere that could put me in more pain

I don't want to roll this dice,
I've seen teenagers in high school commit to the noose
I'm so broken, I feel I might be that too
I'm not much of a fighter

I see a lot of that happens on TV
Over petty drama, BS, I don't want that to be me
Especially in my city
Baltimore is known for its tragedies
Most people walk around with M-16s
So what if another one gets clipped?
What I look at the wrong person the right way
And get shot

I'm not ready
I don't want to go
I'd rather stay home
Maybe it's better to be a bum than risk being dead

But you won't let me
You tell me to get out of bed
You tell me that if I want success I have to make it
But my heart tells me I can't do it
I put strangers on high pedestals
I instinctively assume anyone is better than me
So what if I can't match the standards of these people?

What if I'm considered an outcast again?
I don't want to be hated for being myself again
I don't want to be everyone's punching bag again
I don't want school
It's stressful, aren't a billion tests a year enough?

I barely passed middle school
How could I make it in high school?
I can't go, I don't want to go
But you're motivation says I have to so
As I slowly materialize your fantasy into my reality
I know that my choices in my life don't matter
I am to be the picture that you wanted to give birth to
So my future will be yours to have control over
In High School

Fragmented Mirror

How can you look at yourself without seeing your flaws
Everyone tells me I'm something
I'm incapable of seeing
Cus everyday I wake up, I see that same guy in the
mirror
The same guy who was hated for being himself
When other people were just like him
Like I got hated for liking the same things y'all do

Just because I was a chubby kid
The one you didn't want to be around
Cus despite his positivity
It reflected bad on you
So I reflect on me

I see cracks of my younger days in my reflection
Questioning why I was always an outcast
Why people spoke me out the way
Why I was never the type to be worked with
Why my efforts could never be appreciated

Then high school came along
High school is showing me that my bad past shouldn't
reflect on my character
I stood tall against those who tried to hold me down
Till annual parties come around I see them
On halloween but it's funny
For a day that celebrates wearing masks
I don't remember my praise

It's a holiday to remind me of the ones
responsibility for my low self esteem
How do you face the source of your problems without
cracking?
Being near them was more uncomfortable than nails
on a chalkboard
Cracking my identity, like glass, I shattered

I thought I was someone who was improving but
Being around them brought the child in me back
The one who never spoke, the one who was on the
sidelines
I became a spectator in my own life
Watching myself at this party through the third person
This house party feel like the classrooms

I can't be here
My anxiety kick in with every glare that meets with
mine
The eye contact blinks me to a time I was ridiculed and
criticized
How do I confront the source without cracking
As I forge my own identity
I find it hard to build of my foundation
Of my insecurities, my issues
How do I find a solution to myself without cracking?
I look in the mirror and question
How do I see myself? Instead of my inner child?

Cut Down

I was 7
Red and white tiles
Clippers and smoke
Left subjected to the rough hands of men
A sensitive kid couldn't handle

These men cutting the afro
Puffing cigarette smoke down my throat
Expecting me not to move
"Stay still, boy"
The man held me in place
Father never stayed long enough
To watch them treat me so badly

He'd leave as he does
And leave his son in the dungeon of beasts
He was no fighter

His mother taught him it was okay to cry
That emotions are what makes a man
A human
Not a weakling

But emotions here made me weak
They cut my hair of wool
With sheers made to kill the sheep
My naps were put to rest

By a man who gripped my skull
Another man who bent it to the side
Like an analog stick
But this wasn't a game

That chair was the entrance to a horror movie
Except I lived to tell the tale
The alcohol burned trauma into my hairline
The bald spots
Spoke the story of the man
Who clipped
My ancestral heritage

Watched tears fall out my eyes
But told that boy to "Hush all that crying"
As men don't cry
But the river flowed regardless

Till the well ran dry
My father noticed the tears
And told me
"You'll be ight"
Like you didn't toss the soul of an angel
To the heart of hell

Mother complained about the men who messed up my
afro
Every man after did worse after worse
So how am I supposed to be face
The red and white tiles now?
How does a bishop
Face a pawn of hell directly?

Till the boy finally was given a chance
To choose his own barber
He chose a woman
As men have never been careful
With the boys hair.

Procrastination

These are what my grades say to me

You could never get good grades
You're incapable of giving it your all
How are you a failure
When you're born for success?

Maybe an A isn't what you need
Maybe you just want to get by
You just want to get to the point
Where you're happy?

You've lived by your mothers expectations
There's no such thing as happiness for you
But an A
Can bring you so much peace
knowing you're succeeding
In being the man your mother wants you to be

Cus she never got to go to college
You acknowledge her expectations
May come off as harmful
But it comes from a place of love
Every mother wants best for her child
But you think she wants the worse for you

To cover your face with a mask
Work in the medical field
You're scared you'll resent your creator

So as an act of rebellion
You don't achieve an A
Maybe if you don't go 100%
You'll still have bits of individuality, you won't

Work harder to achieve me or you fail
It's that simple
Like your mother's expectations,
Procrastinator

Isolation

My mother put me in a room with you
As a child
Cus I reminded her too much of my father
My mother had you while she was with him
As men never had the ability
To make my mom feel seen

So when she gave birth to a male
She questioned the world why they gave
Her something that never helped her
As I was passed the gift of isolation

It was more present than my mother
With her in the room next to me
With her own isolation not wanting to be seen
Don't get me wrong my mother wasn't a bad person
But isolation was my sibling growing up

I learned to live with my own
As she had with hers
You've been my best friend before people were an option
As playing on my own
Was more fun than those who would rather
Act impulsively around me

Couldn't handle losing
But yelling was something they could win at
As anger was aimed towards me
The bullet stunned me
I couldn't help but stand there
Take round after round
With no bullet in sight
As it's just me

But I remembered, I couldn't move as I got scolded
I molded into muted clay
With a strong structure
But let the river run down
My faulty foundation will show
Don't cry

If you cry
Isolation turns to a sad space
Than a happy home
But they'd always yell like how my mom has
With men who made her more alone

I sought isolation more than anything
As the sound turned the house to
A mime
So my mom got me a speech therapist
But I could never speak
My room always had me on mute
While my head was on blast

Wishing the yelling would quiet down
That the volume could turn down
That everyone could disappear
My own voices got louder the more there were
I've always hated yelling
But it's always helped me cope

Though I didn't just want inner voices
I learned to start blaming myself for everything
That every shout sounded out that
I was the problem
And was never offered a solution
Which leads me back to isolation

I started to need it more
I wanted my isolation on a grand scale
Where judgement had no bias
I wanted everyone Thanos snapped
I wanted to finally have quiet

Cus I would never yell at myself
A world where isolation is a priority
Where peace is achieved
The sirens turned to crickets
Even if for a minute

But forget that I don't have power over the world
Only myself
My isolation
As I sheltered these homewreckers away from me
Never telling them to stay away
But to stay at a distance
Where I can be alone

I don't want these people in my space
Cus I'm used to being in my own world
As isolation is the only thing that's made me
Feel less alone

Project Boy

Project Boy comes from
Broken beer bottles on the concrete
No freshly lawned grass.
I've seen grass turn grey
Fading into despair to match its environment
Cus flowers respect how you take care of them

But how do you do that?
When the owner can barely take care of themselves
I've lived with broken people here
Where those who never made enough had enough to
move here
That's when I learned what community was

When smiling symbolized healing
That or a temporary distraction
No marble walls, red carpets, chandeliers
I wish I had it as nice as you

I lived believing everyone had it better than me
But living lower class made me humble
I learned to never shoot myself down,
To aim higher
I'm more than a Project boy

But since I moved here,
Parents were scared to have me around
They feared a child of innocence and purity
Would bring cockroaches
That I was a liability
Never wanted to take responsibility
Neglectful of a sensitive child
Who was heartbroken
That he'd been seen as nothing more
Than a reflection of his stereotypical- environment

J Part 1

We were two broken souls
Looking to be repaired
But only broke from pieces into fragments
As we lost each other in our grasp
I was broken when I found you

Freshly out of a break up
Trying to put myself together
When you assisted me
When I first met you digitally
Two strangers brought by a connection
We transferred to reality

Where our personalities clashed more
Than a Ying yang
Yet regardless of difference
Opposites attract more than
Two positives
As good conversation kept our
Connection stable

As I watched a beautiful woman
Feed me sushi
You were my first exposure to this deep feeling
Called love

Till you told me you were in a relationship
My reality shattered knowing I just got out of one
I stepped back knowing there was no
Moving forward with you
To stay in a place where we could be mutual

But I don't understand
The feelings I have for you
Weren't gone just suppressed
I started noticing patterns with your texts
You smiled more when you talked on the phone
The same smile that I wanted when we spoke

My suppression turned jealousy
My insecurities told me
That I was incapable of being loved
My jealousy turned suppression again

Until, you held my hand weeks after you told me
I had never held hands with so much passion
I questioned, you mentioned
Nervousness was the factor
The force leading to our hands attracting
It felt like a connection
But our strings weren't tied yet

Months later, you came by on Christmas
Fate sowed us closer
As you were drawn to me
And kissed me on the cheek
Without a mistletoe in sight

Meaning that night you kissed me
Without your boyfriend in mind
I was drawn closer to the mess
I was drawn closer to you
As the complexities of our relation
Began to escalate

I can't live up to you

I can't live to the idea of you
Being more than what I am now
Loving myself
My flaws, my insecurities
I'm not sure how you'll be able to do it

Accept who you are as an individual
Where do you get that love from?
I want to become a greater version of myself
Who has clarity on his future
His desires

Someone who doesn't let their
Past define their character
That's all I can ever do
Middle school is so deep in my roots
I can't grow into a better version of myself
I'm a broken seed
Hoping I can find growth in the path
My mother forged for me

To be an RN
When right now, I can't decide what I want
In the next hour
I wish I could skip forward in time
To a better version of myself

Where my insecurities will disappear
Where the fat on my body
Doesn't push others away
Where my voice is deeper
Be more masculine
But where I am, I can't live up to you
Maybe one day

Accountability

Your past cannot define you forever
There's a point in time
Where you have to take matters
Into your own hands
And find the better you within yourself

Sophomore Year:
Wonderful Distraction

Rose Tinted Glasses

The responsibilities of a future weigh
Heavy on me
I can't live up to you
I'm in dire need of a distraction
So be it, let it be attraction

Let the feeling of love
Wash over me
Pushing off this heavy burden
Liberate the stress off my brain
I'm tired of thinking of the future

Of who I have to be
Or how I have to live
I want to learn to love myself
Through the love of others
Otherwise, I'm incapable of self acceptance

I'm a failure who can't live up to
The idea of you
But maybe if I love
I'll grow to be you one day

The B Word

I won't ever call a woman the B word
Cus they're human too

Lymphatic Metal

Faulty codes have me work in a weird way
Rejection to my offer
To be your personal robot
Makes me work how we're supposed to
Cus rejection
Has always reminded my body
To accept how things are

That we won't move forward
That stepping away from being your
Ideal model
Is for the best
But why can't it be me?

Most guys you tell me about
Share the same code
Dread head, tall, dark skinned like
They were born on the sun
Like they're your guiding light
But the same reason yours gets extinguished
So why can't I reignite it?

Why can't I be the robot that gives you
Your humanity back?
Let your tears flow into my programming
So I know this is how you hurt
So I know this is how I help you

I don't want to see you hurt by another boy
So maybe give this robot a chance
Cus I know that I won't want to hurt you
That it's not in my programming
That I've had so much history with you
But you don't want a connection
You'd rather keep making history
Than settle for the future
Than settle for a robot

Hopeless Romantic

I'm in love with you
I love your voice
It's a symphony of angels
You're a goddess in my eyes
A seraphim the way I hold you on a
Pedestal higher than me

You're the greatest
Almost too good to be true
You're my national treasure
To a world that is you

You're perfection
Your skin as smooth as cocoa butter
Your fragrance is fatal for falling in love with you
Was a fault of mine I'll never say sorry for

You're everything I would want from a person
But why do you want me?
I'm really not all that special
So why would perfection fall in love with ordinary?

Shouldn't you be with someone
Better suited for you?
Why would a goddess settle for a mortal
Instead of a god?
Why would a queen fall for a civilian
Instead of a King?

I'm a nobody, easily overlooked
I can't see myself giving you
Everything you'd want
I'm so deep in love
I'm confusing this girl I love for a woman

My mentality isn't shaped for high school
A man is supposed to provide
But I can't give you the world
How could I give you yourself?

I can't give you the feeling you give me through
purchases
You're priceless, everything I want but can't commit to
Cus as much as I love you, I can't love myself

My self-esteem is at a all time low
My toxic masculinity keeps me from doing so
The love I want to give you is
Something only a man can provide

I want to take you on flights for our love to soar
I want to give you a smile that's as constant as
mornings
You're my sun but I'm always mourning
To the thought that I can't have you
As you're out of my reach

I feel that all of me won't be enough for you
That once you find someone new
I'll be forgotten

Hopeless Romantic pt. 2

My love for you won't be timeless Cus it was temporary
When I'm lost in your memory
But I love that you're so perfect
You won't even let me hold you back
Which is why
I won't hold you down

I'm not one to stay committed to your whole life
We're only teens
You've got your life
As I've got mine
Too much life to stay committed to one at a time

I feel I'm starting to lose love for you
As my emotions self sabotage seeking ways to let
you go
To let me know that my love is over
That my love is temporary

But I don't know why I feel this way
I put you high on my pedestal
But I think you can be someone else's queen
Find your own King

Find a god to match your holiness
Find someone who can give you the world
Cus I'm losing feelings knowing that
It'll take a long time to give you everything I'd want to
give you

And I won't subject perfection to patience
You should find someone else
Who can give you everything
Cus as much as I know you want to move forward
My love is a dead end

False Heart

I'm in attraction with you
Maybe it's just my inner Pisces speaking
But I can sense you have issues bothering you
That brings me closer to you

I have this issue when it comes to love
I can't quite say that I am with you
Cus as much as I enjoy you as a person
I love the concept of you more than the execution

But, I still want to give you my everything
Spend as much money to invest in a stable foundation
for you
Enough time for us to step into your life
I can't imagine being in your boots
With how heavy your past is

When I offer my assistance you ask me
"Why do you do so much for me?"
I feel a responsibility to be here for you
I love you
Trauma brings people together more than love

But unfortunately, as you start to improve

Our sessions must end

As I can't be a therapist to someone who doesn't need it

You're better

You no longer need me to help you

Too Big A Pedestal

I idolize girls as women
They've always been on a high pedestal
I internalized this idea they could fix everything
Cure my Insecurities, self doubt, boredom, pain
I forget
Women are human too

I can't expect them to love me
When I don't love myself
Let alone know what love is
But throughout the years
I've learn that love
Can be acceptance, compromise
I've had to do both

With the fact
That I can't be perfect

No Closure

To the girl who left
A part of me is waiting for you
When most of me has moved on
Cus I still crave answers
Why did you leave me?

I know I fell too hard
For a talking stage in a month
But I saw a whole life for us
We spoke like we were together
What drove us apart?

I couldn't tell the difference between
Late PM and Early AM
Talking to you
Sleeping on the phone with you
Your presence transcended calls
Made you feel like you were here

You'd correct me
On pronunciation
That I'd mess up on purpose
Cus I loved your accent
Your tongue spoke Latin decent
I've never been a fan of history
But feelings toward you
Would've drove me to being
Your personal historian

What drove us apart?

J Part 2

I'll never forget the first time
She slept on me
I knew that for the first time
I allowed her to feel comfortable
To let her guard down
And feel protected

I never really cared much about
Her public display
That fake shit you put on your face
Was never real to me
Most guys prefer
Societies doll
Than a human

Going in with the right people
With the wrong expectations
But I prefer you in her rawest form
I like to see what's behind the mascara

I look at your face
As you lay on my chest
I feel our inconsistent breathing patterns
As I try to match yours

Appreciating the curves of your lashes
Knowing you appreciate mine
I never knew holding a goddess
Could feel so divine

Sublime stretch marks across your waist
The color fading from your nails
Reveals their clarity
It's clear to me
I love your imperfections
More than your efforts to be perfect

It doesn't work
For as much as a goddess as you are
You're human too
Your grip on my shirt gets tighter
Holding me
Like we're the only people in our galaxy
The last thing I want is space

I won't let you go
Rubbing your back
To remind you I have it
I love seeing you calm
I've been so accustomed to you being angry
Upset at the littlest things
Then get mad at me
But knowing you'll seek refuge in my arms
Remind me that it's worth it
Even though you aren't mine

J Part 3

She told me
Polyamorous meant
What we were doing was fine
The intimacy, okay
Your boyfriend didn't need to know
About us being friends with benefits
It didn't feel okay
I felt I was betraying someone I didn't know

Cus if the roles were reversed
Guilt would haunt me
Knowing he wishes his arms were around you
While mine are
That every kiss we share
He's thinking about giving you

It was long distance
I could understand why you'd feel deprived
Of love and passion
But why did it have to me when you easily
Could told me no

I was freshly 16
Never exposed to an ounce of intimacy
You exposed me to the whole package
And I shouldn't have given you mine
Giving something I could never get back
To someone who didn't deserve it

My friends told me I was misinformed
That polyamorous meant communication
Not disclosed information
I brought up the idea of a conversation
Maybe I could get this guilt off my conscience
If we told him what we were doing

I know you felt anxiety wash over you
Fear you'd get caught up
So you told me no
That we should end
And that's when you took another break
From me

I was left to guess I was the problem
For your absence
If I didn't go through maybe I'd still have you
I have this dependency on you
I can't let go off

That as much as I needed you,
you didn't need me
I spent nights sacrificing sleep
Scared I'd receive another image
Of your palm cut with the pocket knife
The red stained sink
I was worried if I wasn't there it'd happen again
You'd be gone

But you left without a second thought
With you being the first of mine
I couldn't keep tabs on your well being
I spent nights crying over you
Hoping you'd come back but you sent me
On a lust rush

Maybe if I could have the feeling you gave me with
someone else
I could get over you
Cus I can't let this pain get to me any longer
I don't want to mourn you

Impulsive Lust

A friend of 6 months
Ended because of my lust
I've let the feeling corrupt my mind
With no J, I wanted someone else to make me
Feel as good as she made me

You were down for the idea of intimacy
We spoke and we took it
Treating our friends with benefits
As a relationship

Spend a day together
Movies, mall
It was fun but
Every time we'd share a drink
I didn't want it

I didn't know this is what intimacy would lead to
Why my feelings felt so complex
I didn't have enough exposure with J
To know things could turn this way
It didn't make sense

You'd ask me why I didn't like you
I couldn't bring myself to
Naturally I wasn't attracted to you
And I didn't know how fucked up that was
I didn't know you were a rebound

I just wanted to stop feeling pain
From losing a friend of 3 years
I thought if I had the feeling
She gave me from someone else
It'd cancel out the pain

I didn't know it'd come at the cost of losing you
But for as good as you're doing now
Maybe it's better if we don't cross paths again
You didn't deserve what happened between us
I need to be better

Intimate Foundation

My mom raised me better than using a woman
That's why I couldn't be with you anymore
It was bad enough
Our foundation was intimacy
Where we sought companionship
We found a situationship

I didn't know that was a bad thing
Maybe I could salvage a friendship
From sex
I want to keep you around more
But my emotions contradict that
I got embarrassed with you in public
Believing strangers silently spoke
About us

Cus we knew nothing about each other
I don't think we should've
I think it was better how we left things off
After all, I'm a hypocrite for saying men
Shouldn't use you for your body
When I was doing it

I blame myself for going through with your choice
What should've been a stop at my place
For your bus stop
Turned to an evening of lust
My mom says it's not my fault you presented yourself
to me
I believe it's my fault
For going through with it without a second thought

I can't look back on us without a feeling of guilt
rushing over me
You didn't deserve this
You didn't deserve a boy who thought
His good intentions
Would justify his bad

So when I told you we should end
That I was a terrible guy
I deserved that "Fuck you"
Cus I hated myself too
For what I did to you

J Part 3.5

You are toxic
I was a sponge
Soaking your acid
Our connection was radioactive
Acidic to my purity

I spent time wishing I was who I
Was before you
But still thinking about you
I'd daydream
Missing your verbal abuse
I missed when you hurt me
It was the normalcy between us

Cus when I held you
It felt like it was worth the torment
You were troubled
I witnessed it first hand
When yours was cut with your
Knife collection

I found myself dependent on you
As I felt you were dependent on me
That maybe if I wasn't there
You'd look for the red beneath your
Beautiful black skin

I justified actions with trauma
It costed me my innocence
Something I can never obtain again
Part of me wished I saved it for another

But maybe it's better this way
A reminder that it's not wise to give yourself to those
who don't deserve it
You told me you felt obligated
As if I never listened to you?

I was your puppet to control
Never the ventriloquist
My emotions were yours to control
I'd never go against you
Otherwise, why would I live in your toxicity
For 3 years?

Regardless, I don't regret us
I won't
Cus despite how we ended
I'm appreciative of our experience
Even if it hurt me
You taught me pain I'll never forget
I wish you the best

Junior Year: Reflection

Lost Divinity

Christianity was presented
As if God told his followers
To force his teachings down my throat

My sisters father
Told me that if I didn't go to church
I was doomed to be a sinner
That my mother
That as much as constellations
Shaped her beliefs
Was a sinner too

I felt forced listening to his lecture
I believed that I had to respect my elders
But my elders didn't respect me
This man didn't even respect my mother

He brought harm with his arm to her
You think a church can erase the scars
You brought to my mom?
The words God bestows to you
Only pushes my spirit away from him

His messenger used Christianity
To seek redemption for his sinful actions
Hoping it'd get the accountability off his chest

My father is also a believer of christ
He believed I was better off
Dropping out high school
To attend a Christian one
Like an academic baptism
Is this a right an absent father is
Entitled to?

It's Ironic
One thing God and my father have in common
They're both figures I can't comprehend

You never wanted to be a one
You wanted to leave that responsibility to another
Even suggesting the idea that
I abandon my community
To be apart of one
That resides in the embrace of Christ
Shouldn't even be an idea in your head

Funny thing amongst all 3 fathers
Is they didn't have one
And the 2 in my life
Would rather their kids look to him
Than them

This kept my spirit at a standstill
Between what's real and what's isn't
I don't want to seek redemption
For past actions
Cus holy grounds can't be for me
If they're being forced on me

From telemarketers who'd leave
The responsibility of their children
To a figure they look up to
It's funny how my own father
Would insist on letting his son
Learn the teachings of another man
Cus he couldn't teach me anything

Couldn't be enough of one to raise his own son
My soul doesn't seek a belief to
Reside in
But maybe the right person
Can give me a push in the right direction

No room to fly

I never knew how flies felt in cobwebs
Until I got caught tethered to my mom's
Strings of success

Her webs became tangled with my mental
Her strings turned me into a puppet
As I spoke her dreams out
As if I dreamt them

I know she never meant to control me
She always saw me as an extension of her
She wanted me to be more than that
She wanted me further
She thought this fly could be a spider

Extend the webs
Turn these cobwebs to
A family heirloom
Pass down success like silk
Easy to grasp
Wrap your children with it in a cocoon
Pray that they become a spider too
But mom, I want to soar

I don't want to be tied down to these webs
They'd only make me miserable
I thought this is what I needed
To ascend
But I was brought down by my lack of motivation

All flap no height
Saying I wanted to be that RN
But I never saw myself fly for it

Now, I want to be out these webs
Find my seat amongst the clouds
Even when my skies turn grey

Cus I know
That I'm meant to ascend them
I'll find my seat amongst the cosmos

I want to fly where no one has ever gone
Find my own source of happiness
Cus I can't find that
If I'm stuck here

I was never meant to be a spider
I was always supposed to fly
You've cared for me for 17 years
But it's about time
I web my own future together

Self-Love

I acknowledge I don't need love to love myself
I've spent years believing I did
That someone else's love would be
Enough
Where I didn't need any for myself
My forgiveness is the love I give myself

Senior Year: Next Stage

Father

I saw my father the other day
And I felt confusion
He came by with my Christmas gift
Days after Cus he's never been the type to be on time

But nonetheless he brought it
A gaming controller and a $75 gift card
I should've felt happier that he brought it
But I wasn't

I felt like I didn't need him to get it for me
That he's been so absent that a gift from him
Doesn't have the emotional value it should

I wish I had more time with my father
I remembered
He missed so many important points in my life
I was 16 when I got my permit
He missed it
Offered to take my driving
But we drifted apart

Now I drive with a years worth of experience
And he missed it
He missed my senior inauguration
As I performed for my school
The thought of that man being in crowd
Never came by

As I remembered that I don't need you in my life
But I wish I did
I wish you could've been there for my prom
But you're always too busy working
To see the son you worked up

Mom told me before I was born
You announced to the world you were going to be a
father
But after I was born you didn't want to be one

You abandoned your family for another one
And had another kid in between
Your lies formed connections
As mine was severed with my brother
When his mother got fed up with your fibs

And I've accepted the man you are
As you've missed these points in my life
You missed your boy become a man
As he slowly grew up knowing he
Couldn't rely on his father to come around

Now you've set the foundation
For how a man should be for him
The opposite of you

And it's sad Cus you were fun
You were always a jokester
You always tried to relate to your son with sports
Not knowing that I wasn't into them

Despite the amount of times I told you
It was through one ear and out the other
Cus halfway
Your mind couldn't process that transaction

So you kept pushing for a connection
That we could never keep stable
As I saw you the other day
I wanted to cry
Knowing I don't need my father
When every kid should

Every kid should want to rely on their father
Have one that's present
That stays a parent and makes it apparent
That they'll be around
They'll stay

But I never had that
So looking at you
Just reminds me of how much
I wanted to see you more

I love you, dad
And mom tells me you're embarrassed
And if I was in your shoes too, I would be too
As our souls haven't had the space and time to bond

I know you wish you tried more for me
But regardless of your tries
At least we're tied through similarities
We can't keep our rooms clean
As both of our lives have been a mess

But when bridges burnt in our lives
I tried to repair them
As you drowned in the water between
So many times that you've landed in a cycle
Where you run away from your problems

Like you ran away from your family
As you ran away from me and mom
And mom had a tough time raising me
She often saw you in her son
And I don't blame her
I blame you for making our life that way

Regardless, I still love you
After all
If I didn't love you
I wouldn't love myself
That as much as you're a reflection of unreliable
I'm a reflection of you

But I have enough awareness to acknowledge
My cracks as flaws
That I can turn this mirror to new glass
That by the time I'm done with this
You will see me as a reflection of myself

But dad, when I walk across that stage I know
You won't be there
Cus when you can no longer
See the father in the son
It'll be too much to see

Broken Mirror

Growing up is realizing
A mirror isn't broken when it's shattered
Only when there's nothing to reflect

I thought my mirror was broken
I never saw who I am now, only before
I saw a child staring back at me
With the same mask worn to hide his
Insecurities

You could see a tear falling from beneath
As he refused to see a version of himself
He never thought possible

Growing up is realized
My mirror was never broken
It didn't reflect who I was then
It reflected my soul

It reflected the origin of my insecurities
Restricting me from making an identity and now
I see myself
As I reflect on young man I see now

Senior

As I walk towards the step to graduation
Adulthood, manhood
I realized
I never needed a father

The child in me
Wishes he was around more
Maybe I'd know how to ride a bike
A father that'd tend to me
When I fell off

Encourage me to try again
Tell me it was okay to cry
As long as I don't waste my tears
Turn them into fuel
To drive me to do better

I wish my father could've been a man
Maybe I'd love sports more
Maybe I'd connect with most guys more

My father was the type
To tell me we'd watch them together
Just to leave me with the TV
While he was off being MIA
Even while present you were absent

I don't understand why he wants a connection
As if my birth wasn't an opportunity to make one
And now even know,
I see you struggling to fix
The gap between us

You're disappointed
Ashamed that you couldn't be a father
You couldn't be a man
You want to be enough to a kid
Whose satisfied with the little he's had of you

You want to make up for lost time
I'm trying to make the most of mine
Without you within it

Cus father
I could go 10 lifetimes with you
I rarely have you on my mind
But sometimes on my heart

That's why
I'm appreciative of your support when given
But regardless, your words phase through me like a
ghost
You're hollow to me

And when I walk across that stage
I'm okay with the fact
That you'll be absent in that crowd to
Cus father, I never needed you
To be a son
To be a graduate
To be a man

What's next?

Now what?
The cap and gown have been worn
I've pushed through the barrier
Between tireless nights
To drowsy dawns
I've made it
What now?

Is this the part where I'm supposed to be happy?
I've never been good at appreciating
My accomplishments
It's always just been another
Obstacle to overcome

With college around the corner
This is supposed to be major
But why
I feel happy but I know this won't last

The faces in the crowd are fading as I see them
The screams starting sounding like static
As I disassociate with reality
This ain't a sitcom
This is my life

Why can't I appreciate how far I made it?
Cus I'm supposed to go further
I know I've made it to a point
Where most boys don't make it
From getting aimed at gunpoint

Graduation is my best shot for success
But feels like another day
Even though I know this is the happiest day ever
Maybe less overthinking more feeling

Feel positivity
To remind you that part of you knows
That you deserve this

That stage deserves to have you walk over it
You've come a long way
From people have walking over you
Your mom is crying in that crowd
Knowing her first born won't be subjected
To a statistic
That he's the boy who made it

The one who finally became something when nobody
saw it in him
I'm the boy who cried success
Finally becoming a young man
I can live up to you

www.ingramcontent.com/pod-product-compliance
Lightning Source LLC
Chambersburg PA
CBHW032208040426
42449CB00005B/495